FASCINATED BY THE TURN
OF EVENTS
11TH THROUGH
LET'S JOURNEY TOGETHER
THROUGH THIS CAPTIVATING
HISTORICAL PANORAMA!

OCTOBER 11TH
EXPLORING HISTORY AND FUN FACTS

THE FIRST EPISODE OF SATURDAY NIGHT LIVE AIRS

On October 11th, 1975, something super hilarious happened on TV, kiddo! The very first episode of Saturday Night Live aired, bringing lots of laughs and comedy sketches to people's living rooms. Famous comedians like Chevy Chase, John Belushi, and Gilda Radner made funny jokes and performed silly skits that made everyone laugh out loud!

THIS EVENT TEACHES US THAT LAUGHTER IS THE BEST MEDICINE, MY FRIEND. SATURDAY NIGHT LIVE SHOWED US THAT COMEDY CAN BRING PEOPLE TOGETHER AND MAKE ANY SITUATION A LITTLE BIT BRIGHTER. IT REMINDS US TO NEVER UNDERESTIMATE THE POWER OF A GOOD LAUGH!

WHAT ARE SOME OF THE THINGS THAT MAKE YOU LAUGH THE MOST, AND WHY?

_____
_____
_____
_____
_____
_____
_____

HOW CAN ADDING HUMOR TO OUR DAILY LIVES HELP US FEEL HAPPIER AND MORE CONNECTED TO OTHERS?

_____
_____
_____
_____
_____
_____
_____

NATIONAL DAY OF PATAGONIA (ARGENTINA)

On October 11th, Argentina celebrates the National Day of Patagonia! Patagonia is a region located in the southern part of the country, filled with stunning landscapes, breathtaking mountains, and amazing wildlife. People celebrate this day by showcasing the beauty and culture of Patagonia through festivals, parades, and delicious traditional food. It's a day to appreciate and honor the unique wonders of this remarkable region.

THIS SPECIAL EVENT TEACHES US THAT IT'S IMPORTANT TO CELEBRATE AND APPRECIATE THE BEAUTY OF OUR OWN LAND. JUST LIKE PEOPLE IN ARGENTINA CELEBRATE PATAGONIA, WE SHOULD TAKE THE TIME TO LEARN ABOUT AND VALUE THE UNIQUE FEATURES OF OUR OWN HOMETOWN OR COUNTRY.

WHAT ARE SOME THINGS THAT MAKE YOUR HOMETOWN OR COUNTRY SPECIAL AND WORTH CELEBRATING?

_____

_____

_____

_____

_____

_____

_____

HOW CAN YOU GET INVOLVED IN HONORING AND PRESERVING THE BEAUTY OF YOUR LOCAL ENVIRONMENT IN A FUN AND EXCITING WAY?

_____

_____

_____

_____

_____

_____

_____

_____

ALBERT EINSTEIN TELLS FDR ABOUT A POWERFUL KIND OF BOMB

On October 11th, 1939, something really wacky happened! The super-smart scientist, Albert Einstein, sent a letter to President Franklin D. Roosevelt, which said that it might be possible to make a super-duper powerful bomb called an atomic bomb! Can you imagine that? Einstein's letter was a big deal because it made President Roosevelt realize that the United States needed to start working on building an atomic bomb too. This crazy idea would change the world forever!

THIS EVENT TEACHES US THAT EVEN THE BRIGHTEST MINDS CAN THINK OF BOTH WONDERFUL AND DANGEROUS IDEAS. EINSTEIN'S LETTER MADE PEOPLE REALIZE THAT ATOMIC BOMBS HAD THE POWER TO CAUSE GREAT DESTRUCTION. IT REMINDS US TO ALWAYS CONSIDER THE CONSEQUENCES OF OUR ACTIONS AND THINK ABOUT HOW WE CAN USE OUR INTELLIGENCE FOR GOOD.

IF YOU WERE A SCIENTIST, WHAT INCREDIBLE INVENTION WOULD YOU CREATE TO MAKE THE WORLD A BETTER PLACE?

_____

_____

_____

_____

_____

_____

_____

HOW CAN WE MAKE SURE WE USE OUR INTELLIGENCE AND KNOWLEDGE TO HELP OTHERS INSTEAD OF CAUSING HARM?

_____

_____

_____

_____

_____

_____

_____

_____

SOLIDARITY DAY WITH SOUTH AFRICAN POLITICAL PRISONERS

On October 11th, many people around the world celebrate Solidarity Day with South African Political Prisoners. This is a day to show support for those who have been imprisoned for fighting against inequality and injustice in South Africa. People wear ribbons in the colors of the South African flag to show their solidarity and raise awareness about the ongoing struggle for freedom and human rights.

THIS EVENT TEACHES US THAT IT'S IMPORTANT TO STAND UP FOR WHAT IS RIGHT AND SUPPORT THOSE WHO ARE FIGHTING FOR JUSTICE. SOUTH AFRICAN POLITICAL PRISONERS FACED GREAT CHALLENGES IN THEIR FIGHT AGAINST INEQUALITY, BUT THEY NEVER GAVE UP. THEY REMIND US THAT WE CAN MAKE A DIFFERENCE NO MATTER HOW SMALL WE ARE.

HOW CAN YOU SHOW SUPPORT FOR PEOPLE WHO ARE FIGHTING FOR JUSTICE IN YOUR OWN COMMUNITY?

_____

_____

_____

_____

_____

_____

_____

WHAT CAN YOU DO TO HELP CREATE A MORE EQUAL AND FAIR WORLD?

_____

_____

_____

_____

_____

_____

_____

ETHIOPIAN PRIME MINISTER WINS NOBEL PEACE PRIZE FOR MAKING FRIENDS

Imagine having a best friend you used to fight with all the time. Well, that's what happened between Ethiopia and Eritrea, two countries in Africa. They were like two stubborn kids who just couldn't get along. But then, along came Abiy Ahmed, the superhero-like Prime Minister of Ethiopia. He decided it was time to make peace and be friends with Eritrea. He worked really hard to end the long-standing conflict between the two countries. And guess what? He actually did it! His efforts earned him the prestigious Nobel Peace Prize.

THIS EVENT TEACHES US THAT MAKING FRIENDS AND RESOLVING CONFLICTS PEACEFULLY IS REALLY IMPORTANT. JUST LIKE ABIY AHMED, WE SHOULD ALWAYS TRY OUR BEST TO FIND PEACEFUL SOLUTIONS AND MAKE FRIENDS INSTEAD OF FIGHTING. IT'S LIKE BRINGING CHOCOLATE CHIP COOKIES TO A DISAGREEMENT. YUMMY SOLUTIONS FOR EVERYONE!

IF YOU COULD SOLVE A CONFLICT BETWEEN TWO FRIENDS, HOW WOULD YOU DO IT IN A FUN AND SILLY WAY?

_____

_____

_____

_____

_____

_____

_____

HOW CAN WE BE LIKE ABIY AHMED AND PROMOTE FRIENDSHIPS AND PEACEFUL RELATIONSHIPS IN OUR OWN LIVES? MAYBE WITH A SECRET HANDSHAKE OR A FRIENDSHIP DANCE?

_____

_____

_____

_____

_____

_____

FIRST AMERICAN WOMAN TO WALK IN SPACE

On October 11, 1984, a super cool and adventurous astronaut named kathryn D. Sullivan became the very first American woman to venture out into space. She boarded the Space Shuttle Challenger and floated in the vastness of the Universe, making history! kathryn's remarkable achievement showed the world that girls can achieve anything they set their minds to, even exploring the great unknown.

THIS EVENT TEACHES US THAT DREAMS REALLY DO COME TRUE, AND THAT THERE ARE NO LIMITS TO WHAT GIRLS CAN ACHIEVE. KATHRYN'S AMAZING SPACEWALK INSPIRES US TO DREAM BIG AND STRIVE TO REACH FOR THE STARS, NO MATTER WHAT CHALLENGES WE MAY FACE.

IF YOU COULD GO ON A SPACE ADVENTURE, WHAT PLANET WOULD YOU WANT TO VISIT AND WHY?

WHAT ARE SOME THINGS YOU COULD DO RIGHT NOW TO PURSUE YOUR OWN DREAMS AND MAKE THEM COME TRUE?

IT'S MY PARTY DAY

October 11th is a special day called "It's My Party Day!" It's a day to celebrate your birthday or any special occasion that you want to party for. Get ready to put on your party hat, grab some balloons, and get your dancing shoes on because it's time to have a blast! Whether you have a big party with all your friends or a small celebration with your family, it's a day to have fun and make memories that will last a lifetime.

THIS EVENT TEACHES US THAT IT'S IMPORTANT TO CELEBRATE AND ENJOY SPECIAL MOMENTS IN OUR LIVES. BIRTHDAYS AND SPECIAL OCCASIONS GIVE US A CHANCE TO APPRECIATE THE PEOPLE WE LOVE AND HAVE A GOOD TIME TOGETHER. IT'S A REMINDER TO CHERISH THESE MOMENTS AND CREATE JOYFUL MEMORIES.

IF YOU COULD HAVE ANY THEME FOR YOUR DREAM PARTY, WHAT WOULD IT BE? WOULD IT BE A SUPERHERO PARTY, A MAGICAL UNICORN PARTY, OR SOMETHING ELSE ENTIRELY?

_____
_____
_____
_____
_____

WHAT IS YOUR FAVORITE THING ABOUT CELEBRATING YOUR BIRTHDAY? IS IT THE PRESENTS, THE CAKE, OR SPENDING TIME WITH YOUR LOVED ONES?

_____
_____
_____
_____
_____
_____

LEWIS HAMILTON SPEEDS TO RECORD-BREAKING VICTORY!

Whoosh! On October 11th, the super speedy British Mercedes driver, Lewis Hamilton, zoomed his way to victory at the Eifel Grand Prix held in Germany's Nurburgring. His stunning win not only earned him the glory of being crowned the champion, but also allowed him to equal the legendary Michael Schumacher's record of 91 Formula 1 victories! With lightning-fast reflexes and incredible skill, Lewis showed the world what it means to be a true racing champion!

THIS EVENT TEACHES US THAT WITH DETERMINATION, PRACTICE, AND A LOVE FOR WHAT YOU DO, YOU CAN ACHIEVE INCREDIBLE THINGS. JUST LIKE LEWIS HAMILTON, YOU TOO CAN CHASE YOUR DREAMS AND ACCOMPLISH AMAZING FEATS IF YOU WORK HARD AND BELIEVE IN YOURSELF.

IMAGINE YOU'RE A RACE CAR DRIVER LIKE
LEWIS HAMILTON! WHAT STEPS WOULD YOU
TAKE TO IMPROVE YOUR DRIVING SKILLS AND
BECOME A CHAMPION ON THE RACETRACK?

LET'S DESIGN YOUR VERY OWN RACE
CAR! HOW WOULD YOU MAKE IT SUPER
FAST AND UNIQUE?

COMING OUT DAY

On October 11th, people all over the world celebrate Coming Out Day. This is a day to honor and support individuals who are brave enough to reveal their true selves, especially those who identify as LGBTQ+. It's a day to show love, acceptance, and respect for everyone's unique identities and to create a more inclusive and understanding world.

THIS EVENT TEACHES US THAT IT'S IMPORTANT TO CELEBRATE AND SUPPORT EVERYONE, NO MATTER WHO THEY LOVE OR HOW THEY IDENTIFY. COMING OUT DAY REMINDS US THAT EVERYONE DESERVES TO BE TREATED WITH KINDNESS AND RESPECT, JUST AS THEY ARE.

HOW CAN YOU MAKE SOMEONE FEEL INCLUDED AND SUPPORTED IF THEY SHARE SOMETHING IMPORTANT ABOUT THEMSELVES WITH YOU? FOR EXAMPLE, IF SOMEONE WANTS TO TELL YOU ABOUT THEIR FAVORITE COLOR OR HOBBY?

_____

_____

_____

_____

CAN YOU THINK OF DIFFERENT WAYS TO SHOW KINDNESS AND RESPECT TO SOMEONE WHO MIGHT BE FEELING NERVOUS OR SCARED ABOUT COMING OUT? MAYBE YOU COULD GIVE THEM A FUNNY CARD OR DRAW A HAPPY PICTURE TO MAKE THEM SMILE!

_____

_____

_____

_____

_____

THE EXPLODING PHONES CARNIVAL

Once upon a time, in a land far, far away called South korea, there was a company called Samsung that made really cool phones. One day, they made a special phone called the Note 7 that had all the latest and greatest features. It was shiny, the screen was big, and it had a fancy stylus pen. kids and adults all over the world got really excited about this phone. But uh-oh, there was a big problem! Some of these shiny Note 7 phones started catching fire. Yikes! People got scared and complained about it. So, Samsung did something really important - they decided to stop making the Note 7 phones forever because they wanted to keep everyone safe.

THIS EVENT TEACHES US THAT EVEN BIG COMPANIES CAN MAKE MISTAKES, BUT IT'S IMPORTANT TO ADMIT THEM AND TAKE RESPONSIBILITY. SAMSUNG LISTENED TO PEOPLE'S COMPLAINTS AND MADE THE TOUGH DECISION TO STOP PRODUCING THE NOTE 7 PHONES, WHICH SHOWED THEY CARED ABOUT THEIR CUSTOMERS' SAFETY.

WHAT ARE SOME WAYS YOU CAN TAKE RESPONSIBILITY FOR YOUR OWN MISTAKES AND MAKE THINGS RIGHT?

_____

_____

_____

_____

_____

_____

_____

HOW CAN YOU SHOW THAT YOU CARE ABOUT THE SAFETY AND WELL-BEING OF OTHERS?

_____

_____

_____

_____

_____

_____

_____

INTERNATIONAL GIRL'S DAY

Hooray! It's International Girl's Day, a special day to celebrate and empower girls all around the world. On this day, people come together to recognize the amazing achievements of girls and to highlight the important work that still needs to be done to promote equality and fairness for all. It's a day to honor the mighty girls and remind everyone that girls can do anything they set their minds to!

THIS EVENT TEACHES US THAT EVERY GIRL DESERVES EQUAL OPPORTUNITIES AND RESPECT. INTERNATIONAL GIRL'S DAY REMINDS US TO VALUE GIRLS' VOICES, TALENTS, AND DREAMS JUST AS MUCH AS WE VALUE BOYS'. IT ENCOURAGES US TO SUPPORT AND EMPOWER THE GIRLS IN OUR LIVES, FROM OUR FRIENDS TO OUR SISTERS, SO THEY CAN THRIVE AND MAKE A DIFFERENCE IN THE WORLD.

HOW CAN YOU HELP SUPPORT THE GIRLS IN YOUR COMMUNITY AND MAKE SURE THEY HAVE THE SAME CHANCES TO SUCCEED AS BOYS?

_____
_____
_____
_____
_____
_____
_____

WHAT ARE SOME WAYS WE CAN CELEBRATE THE ACHIEVEMENTS OF GIRLS AND INSPIRE THEM TO REACH FOR THE STARS?

_____
_____
_____
_____
_____
_____
_____
_____

FIRST WOMAN FBI "SPECIAL INVESTIGATOR", ALASKA DAVIDSON, APPOINTED

In the amazing year of 1922, something super special happened! The FBI (which stands for Federal Bureau of Investigation) appointed their very first woman "special investigator" named Alaska Davidson. This was a huge step forward in showing that girls can be just as brave and smart as boys when it comes to solving mysteries and fighting crime!

THIS EVENT TEACHES US
THAT GIRLS HAVE THE POWER
TO DO ANYTHING THEY SET
THEIR MINDS TO, WHETHER
IT'S SOLVING MYSTERIES
OR FIGHTING CRIME. JUST
LIKE ALASKA DAVIDSON,
WE SHOULD BELIEVE IN
OURSELVES AND FOLLOW OUR
PASSIONS, NO MATTER WHAT
ANYONE ELSE SAYS.

IF YOU WERE A SPECIAL INVESTIGATOR LIKE
ALASKA DAVIDSON, WHAT KIND OF MYSTERIES
WOULD YOU WANT TO SOLVE?

HOW CAN WE SUPPORT AND ENCOURAGE GIRLS
AND BOYS TO PURSUE THEIR DREAMS, EVEN IF
THEY FACE SOME OBSTACLES ALONG THE WAY?

THE POPE CALLS FOR A BIG MEETING AT THE VATICAN

On October 11th, 1962, something big happened in Vatican City - the Pope, who is like the boss of the Catholic Church, called for a special meeting called the Second Vatican Council. This meeting was super important because it brought together a bunch of church leaders from all around the world to talk about how to make the Catholic Church even better and more modern.

THIS EVENT TEACHES US THAT IT'S IMPORTANT TO KEEP LEARNING AND GROWING, EVEN IF YOU'RE ALREADY IN CHARGE OF SOMETHING. THE POPE WANTED TO MAKE THE CHURCH BETTER, SO HE CALLED THIS SPECIAL MEETING TO GET NEW IDEAS AND MAKE CHANGES. IT'S A REMINDER THAT NO MATTER WHO YOU ARE, THERE'S ALWAYS ROOM FOR IMPROVEMENT!

HOW CAN YOU MAKE YOUR SCHOOL OR COMMUNITY BETTER? MAYBE YOU CAN THINK OF A FUN EVENT OR A HELPFUL PROJECT TO MAKE THINGS MORE AWESOME!

_____

_____

_____

_____

_____

_____

CAN YOU THINK OF A TIME WHEN YOU HAD TO TRY SOMETHING NEW OR MAKE CHANGES TO MAKE THINGS BETTER? HOW DID IT GO?

_____

_____

_____

_____

_____

_____

_____

_____

NASA'S SPACE SHUTTLE COMPLETES ITS 100TH MISSION

On October 11th, something really cool happened in outer space! NASA's Space Shuttle completed its 100th mission! Can you believe it? The Space Shuttle is like a super fancy bus that travels all the way up in the sky to explore space. It's like a big spaceship with wings that can go up and down, just like a bird! On this special occasion, the Space Shuttle had already taken 100 trips to help us learn more about space, conduct experiments, and even send brave astronauts up there!

THIS EVENT TEACHES US THAT EXPLORING SPACE IS A GREAT ADVENTURE, AND IT TAKES A LOT OF TEAMWORK AND EFFORT. JUST LIKE THE ASTRONAUTS WHO FLY ON THE SPACE SHUTTLE, WE CAN DREAM BIG AND WORK TOGETHER TO DISCOVER NEW THINGS AND MAKE AMAZING DISCOVERIES.

IF YOU COULD GO ON A TRIP TO OUTER SPACE
ON THE SPACE SHUTTLE, WHAT SCIENTIFIC
EXPERIMENT WOULD YOU CONDUCT AND WHY?

HOW DO YOU THINK ASTRONAUTS PREPARE
FOR THEIR TRIPS INTO SPACE? CAN YOU COME
UP WITH A FUNNY AND CREATIVE WAY TO
TRAIN LIKE AN ASTRONAUT?

INTERNATIONAL DULCE DE LECHE DAY

On October 11th, we celebrate International Dulce de Leche Day. Dulce de Leche is a sweet and creamy caramel-like sauce that is made by heating condensed milk. It is used in many delicious desserts like flan, ice cream, and pancakes. On this special day, people all around the world come together to enjoy this delectable treat and share their favorite dulce de leche recipes.

THIS EVENT TEACHES US THAT FOOD BRINGS PEOPLE TOGETHER AND GIVES US A REASON TO CELEBRATE. THE LOVE FOR DULCE DE LECHE UNITES PEOPLE FROM DIFFERENT CULTURES AND BACKGROUNDS, SHOWING THAT WE CAN FIND JOY IN SHARING AND APPRECIATING DELICIOUS TREATS.

WHAT ARE SOME OTHER INTERNATIONAL DESSERTS THAT YOU WOULD LIKE TO TRY AND WHY?

HOW CAN YOU SHARE YOUR FAVORITE DULCE DE LECHE RECIPE WITH YOUR FRIENDS AND FAMILY IN A FUN AND CREATIVE WAY?

JOIN US AS WE UNVEIL THE FASCINATING CHRONICLES OF OCTOBER 12TH'S STORIED HISTORY.

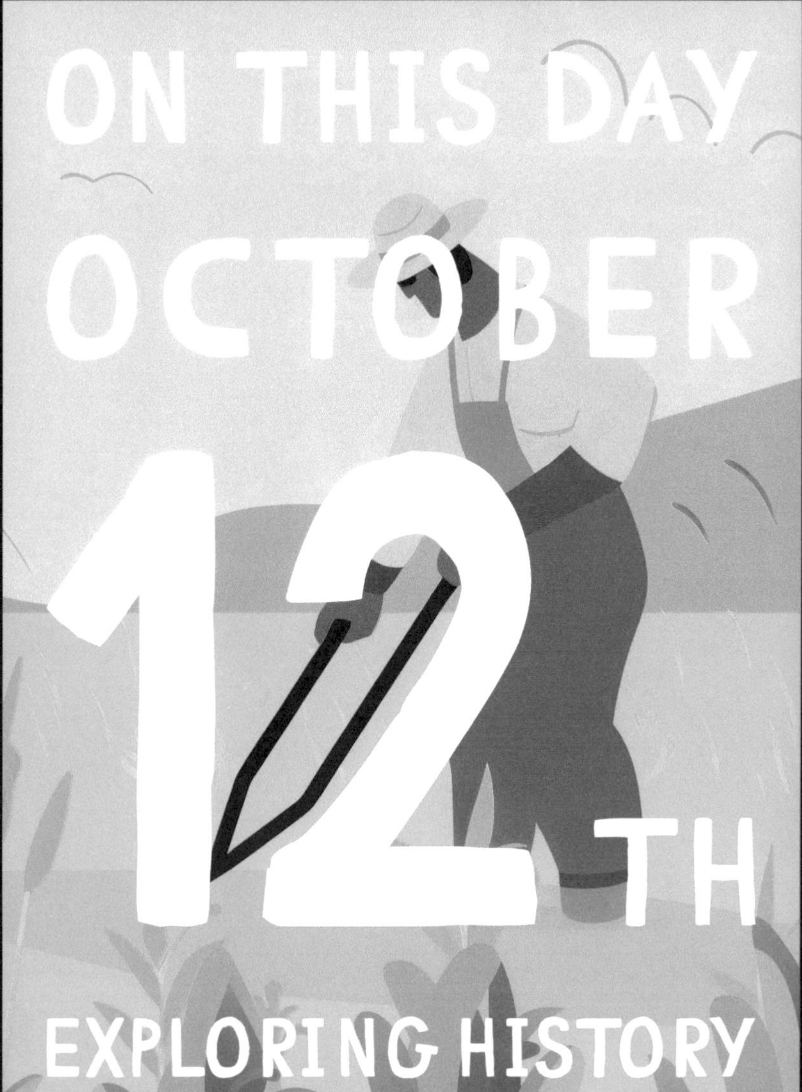
ON THIS DAY
OCTOBER
12TH
EXPLORING HISTORY
AND FUN FACTS

ON THIS DAY
OCTOBER
1ST
EXPLORING HISTORY AND FUN FACTS

ON THIS DAY
OCTOBER
2ND
EXPLORING HISTORY AND FUN FACTS

ON THIS DAY
OCTOBER
3RD
EXPLORING HISTORY AND FUN FACTS

ON THIS DAY
OCTOBER
4TH
EXPLORING HISTORY AND FUN FACTS

ON THIS DAY
OCTOBER
5TH
EXPLORING HISTORY AND FUN FACTS

ON THIS DAY
OCTOBER
6TH
EXPLORING HISTORY AND FUN FACTS

ON THIS DAY
OCTOBER
7TH
EXPLORING HISTORY AND FUN FACTS

ON THIS DAY
OCTOBER
8TH
EXPLORING HISTORY AND FUN FACTS

ON THIS DAY
OCTOBER
9TH
EXPLORING HISTORY AND FUN FACTS

ON THIS DAY
OCTOBER
10TH
EXPLORING HISTORY AND FUN FACTS

ON THIS DAY
OCTOBER
11TH
EXPLORING HISTORY AND FUN FACTS

ON THIS DAY
OCTOBER
12TH
EXPLORING HISTORY AND FUN FACTS

ON THIS DAY
OCTOBER
13TH
EXPLORING HISTORY AND FUN FACTS

ON THIS DAY
OCTOBER
14TH
EXPLORING HISTORY AND FUN FACTS

ON THIS DAY
OCTOBER
15TH
EXPLORING HISTORY AND FUN FACTS

ON THIS DAY
OCTOBER
16TH
EXPLORING HISTORY AND FUN FACTS

ON THIS DAY
OCTOBER
17TH
EXPLORING HISTORY
AND FUN FACTS

ON THIS DAY
OCTOBER
18TH
EXPLORING HISTORY
AND FUN FACTS

ON THIS DAY
OCTOBER
19TH
EXPLORING HISTORY
AND FUN FACTS

ON THIS DAY
OCTOBER
20TH
EXPLORING HISTORY
AND FUN FACTS

ON THIS DAY
OCTOBER
21ST
EXPLORING HISTORY
AND FUN FACTS

ON THIS DAY
OCTOBER
22ND
EXPLORING HISTORY
AND FUN FACTS

ON THIS DAY
OCTOBER
23RD
EXPLORING HISTORY
AND FUN FACTS

ON THIS DAY
OCTOBER
24TH
EXPLORING HISTORY
AND FUN FACTS

ON THIS DAY
OCTOBER
25TH
EXPLORING HISTORY
AND FUN FACTS

ON THIS DAY
OCTOBER
26TH
EXPLORING HISTORY
AND FUN FACTS

ON THIS DAY
OCTOBER
27TH
EXPLORING HISTORY
AND FUN FACTS

ON THIS DAY
OCTOBER
28TH
EXPLORING HISTORY
AND FUN FACTS

ON THIS DAY
OCTOBER
29TH
EXPLORING HISTORY
AND FUN FACTS

ON THIS DAY
OCTOBER
30TH
EXPLORING HISTORY
AND FUN FACTS

ON THIS DAY
OCTOBER
31ST
EXPLORING HISTORY
AND FUN FACTS

Made in United States
Troutdale, OR
11/27/2023

15036626R00040